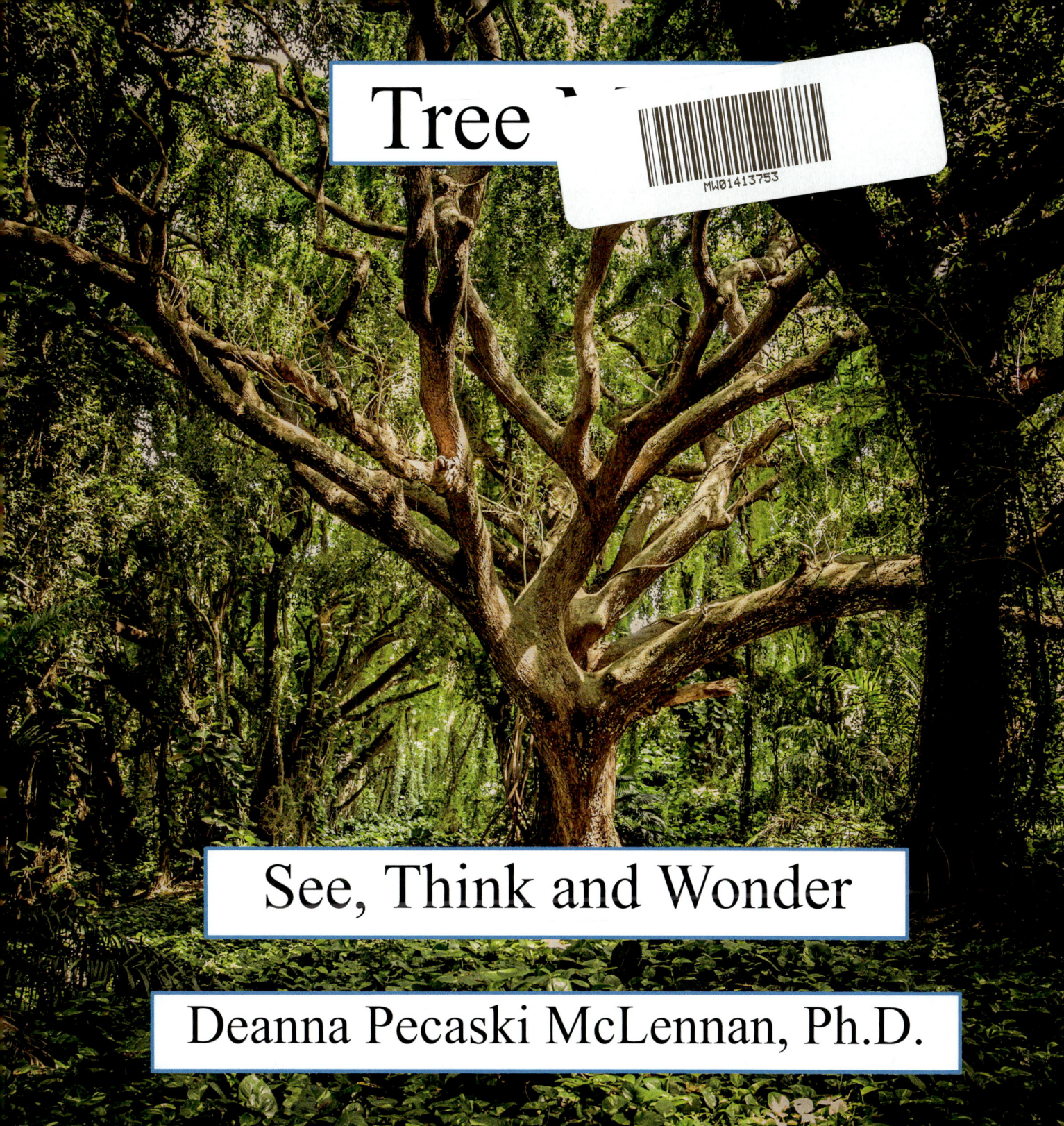

Tree

See, Think and Wonder

Deanna Pecaski McLennan, Ph.D.

For Dana

Copyright © by Deanna Pecaski McLennan
First edition 2022

All rights reserved.

No part of this publication may be reproduced in any form, or by any means, electronic or mechanical, including photocopying, recording, or any information browsing, storage or retrieval system, without permission in writing from the author.

www.mrsmclennan.blogspot.ca

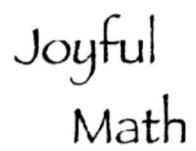

Joyful Math

It is peaceful to spend time in nature. There is so much to discover on the trail. When I explore I often find math in the trees.

I **see** a tire swing.

I **think** it is hanging from a thick branch.

I **wonder** how much weight it can hold.

I **see** many stumps.

I **think** they are about the same size.

I **wonder** if they all come from the same tree.

I **see** a tree canopy.

I **think** it is very high.

I **wonder** how tall are these trees.

I **see** beautiful leaves.

I **think** the weather must be getting colder.

I **wonder** how each tree changes its colour.

I **see** something way up high.

I **think** this kitten is exploring.

I **wonder** how it will travel down.

I **see** juicy apples.

I **think** they are ready to be picked.

I **wonder** how a flower turns into a fruit.

I **see** concentric circles.

I **think** they are growing in size.

I **wonder** why they form in this way.

I **see** a waxy leaf.

I **think** it is repelling the rain.

I **wonder** how the droplets maintain their shape.

I **see** little fungi.

I **think** they are growing in the crevice.

I **wonder** how many grow on this tree.

I **see** many needles.

I **think** they are strong and prickly.

I **wonder** why they do not shed in the winter.

I **see** a delicate nest.

I **think** it keeps the eggs safe.

I **wonder** how the bird constructed it so precisely.

I **see** thick bark.

I **think** it protects the tree.

I **wonder** how it feels on my hand.

I **see** a wide eye.

I **think** an owl might be hiding.

I **wonder** how animals camouflage in trees.

I **see** two arms.

I **think** they are giving a hug.

I **wonder** how big around is the trunk.

I **see** moss.

I **think** it grows in the shade.

I **wonder** how much of it covers this tree.

I **see** streams of light.

I **think** the sun is shining brightly.

I **wonder** why it appears in straight lines.

I **see** gnarled roots.

I **think** this tree is very old.

I **wonder** how it grows above the earth.

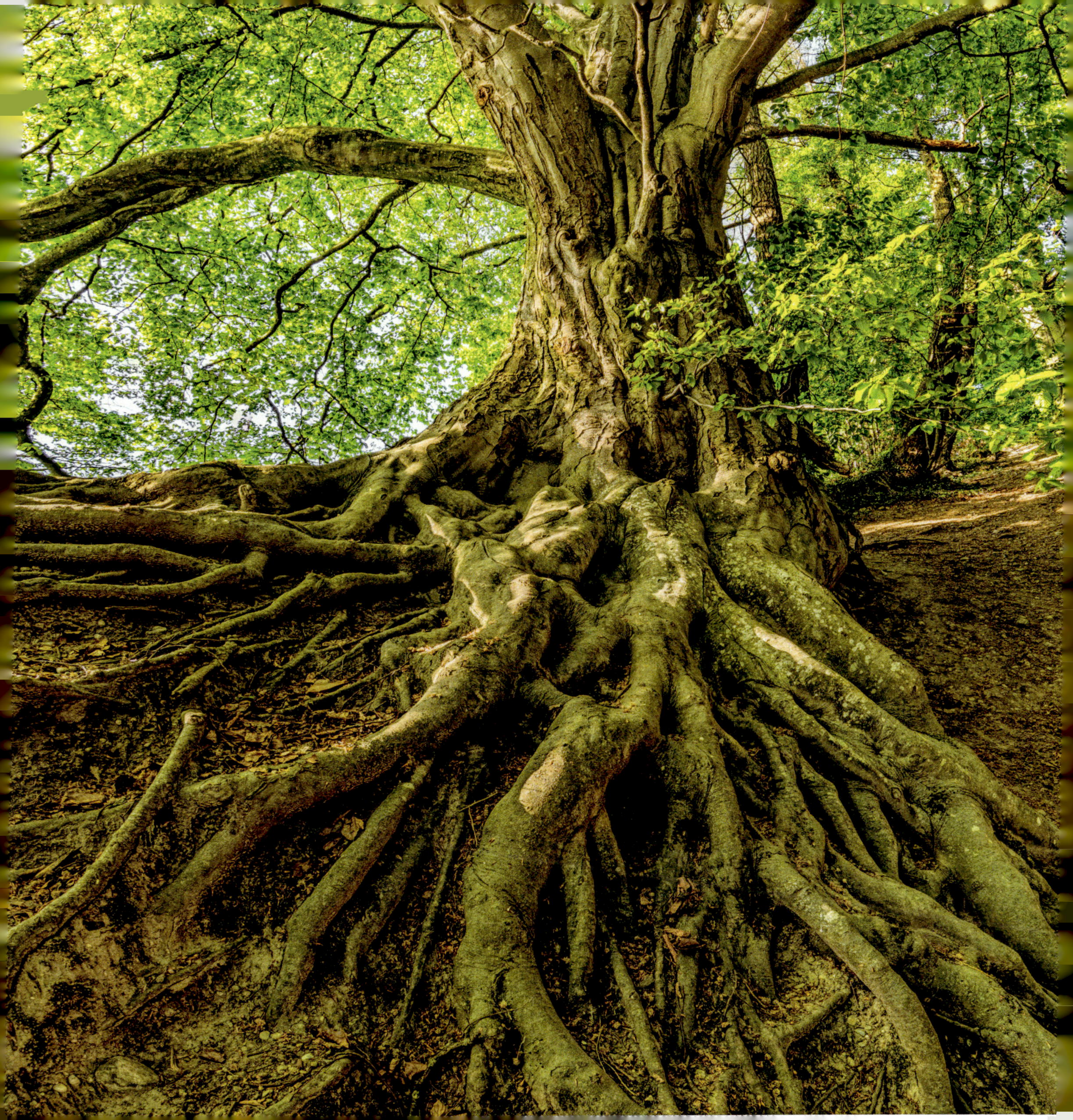

Author's Note

Math is all around us! As an educator I love helping children discover the authentic ways we use math in our everyday lives! As children recognize the integrated, meaningful ways math helps our world work, their interest and confidence in the subject will grow. Exploring the authentic math that exists in our surroundings can help nurture children's interest and confidence, building a strong foundation for subsequent experiences. I love taking math out of 'math class'.

As a kindergarten educator I have always enjoyed helping children discover the rich math that lives in the world around them. Observing and understanding math in the natural environment each day will grow children as mathematicians.

My hope in writing this book is to inspire children, educators and families to see math as an inviting discipline that does not exist in isolation. Exploring math in nature offers countless opportunities for children and adults to make amazing mathematical connections.

This book does not need to be read beginning to end. The photos can be used individually, or in combination, to spark mathematical conversations and connections with children. Ask children what they **see, think and wonder** about each picture. Ask what their theories are for what they see happening on each page. Adults can support and extend children's mathematical and scientific ideas by asking them to share their observations using the see, think, wonder routine.

The information presented in this book can serve as an introduction to new math concepts, or as a reference when mathematical concepts are discovered by children as they explore their surroundings (e.g., patterns on the tree's bark, the angle of branches). You might choose to use only the photos as conversation starters one at a time, or read the book in its entirety using all photos and narratives. The possibilities are endless!

When we look at the world through a mathematical lens, we discover that anything is possible!

-Deanna

How to Use This Book

This book can be read to children using the '**see, think, and wonder**' sentence starters that correspond to each picture. Ask children to consider the mathematical prompts on each page, and hypothesize about how they might research the inquiry that is presented.

This book can also be shared with children using only the photos. Present each photo to children one at a time. Engage children in a mathematical conversation using the see, think, and wonder routine as they explore the photos.

At first children can be invited to carefully observe each photo and share what they **see**. Ask children to use rich description as they articulate their observations. Next, ask children to make personal connections to the information presented in the text and photos. They can articulate what they **think** about the question prompts in the text, or make inferences about the information shared in the photos. Finally, ask children to share what they **wonder** about the text and photos.

What are children curious about? What do they notice in the foreground, and background of each photo? What connections can they make to the book? What experiences do they have that relate to the objects or situations being presented? Is there something they are interested in learning further? How might they go about conducting mathematical research? What knowledge do they need to have in order to research their question? What tools and supports might help them in their quest? How can they share their findings with others?

This rich mathematical conversation can inspire children to understand what they read, make connections to the book, and inspire inquiry-based learning for deeper exploration and understanding.

After the children have explored the book, consider asking them to co-create their own version of the text. Children can illustrate pictures and write their own narratives. Invite children to look around their homes and communities for other mathematical situations to explore. Perhaps children can digitally document what they find and add these to their own See, Think and Wonder. The possibilities are as endless as the questions children ask.

Deanna Pecaski McLennan, Ph.D., is an elementary educator in Ontario, Canada. Deanna is fascinated by math and loves exploring its natural and authentic application in the living world. She hopes to help children and families recognize math as a beautiful and fascinating subject, and grow children's confidence, accuracy and interest in math.

Follow Deanna on Twitter and Instagram for regular updates including ideas for engaging children in playful, emergent math inside the classroom and beyond. Extending math learning outdoors is a favourite exploration!

Connect with Deanna:

deannapecaskimclennan@gmail.com
@McLennan1977

Also from Deanna

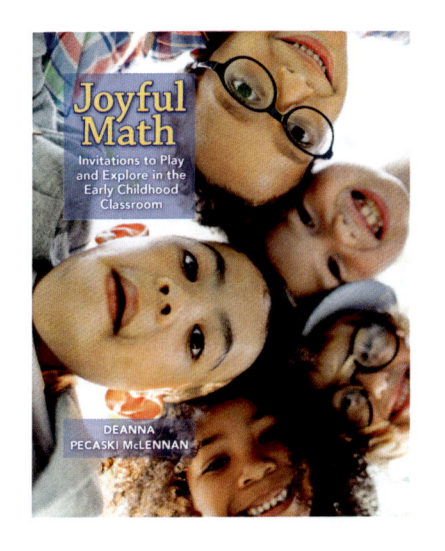

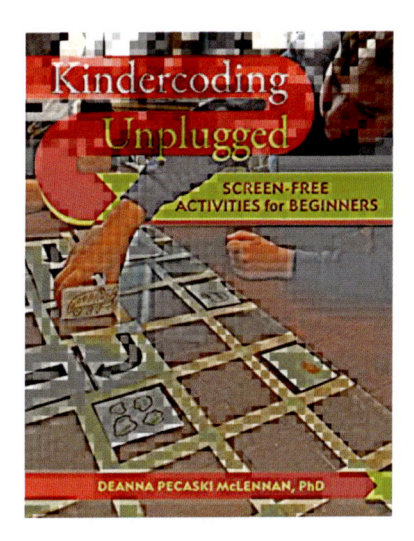

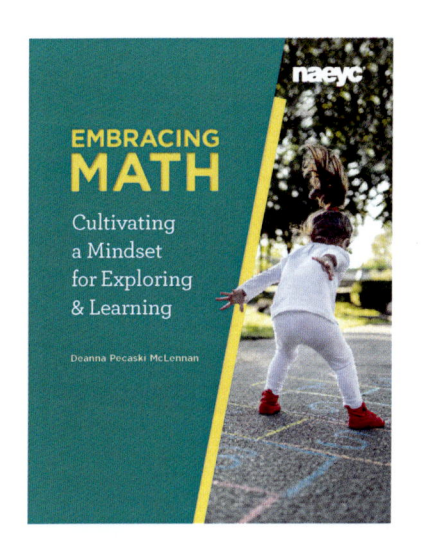

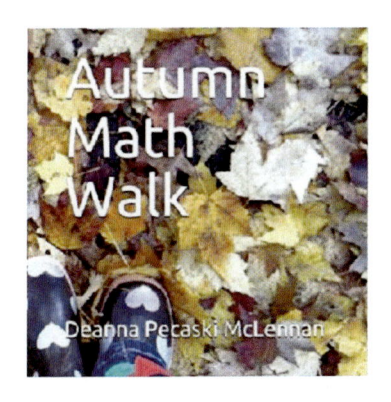

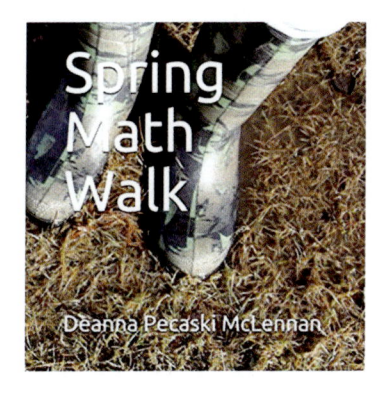

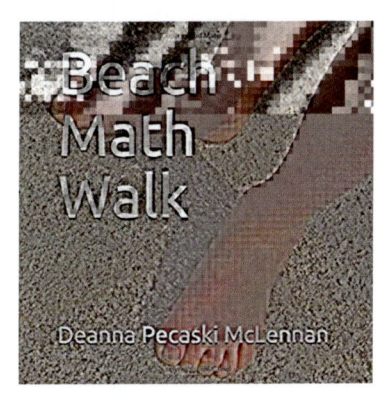

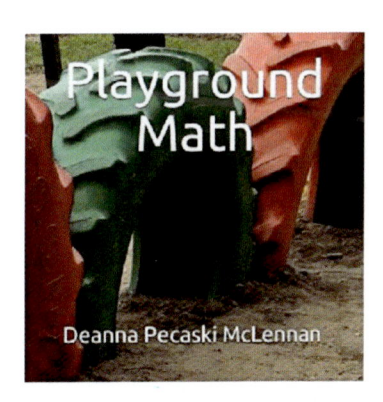

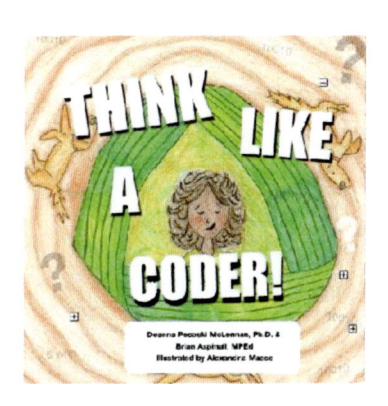

Joyful
Math

Manufactured by Amazon.ca
Acheson, AB